FLIGHT TO FEAR

Tom Belina

A PACEMAKER BESTELLERS™ BOOK

FEARON·PITMAN PUBLISHERS, INC.
Belmont, California

Series Director: Tom Belina
Designer: Richard Kharibian
Cover and illustrations: Cliff Spohn

ISBN–0–8224–5252–2

Library of Congress Catalog Card Number: 77-70252

Printed in the United States of America.

1. 9 8 7 6 5 4 3

CONTENTS

CHAPTER 1

OFF TO JAMAICA

A long line of people waited to get on the airplane. But first each one had to pass through a metal detector. This was to make sure that no one had a hidden gun. Since they had started using metal detectors at airports, the number of hijackings had dropped to almost nothing.

Linda Logan wondered about the red-haired man in front of her. There was something strange about him. Maybe it was his cold blue eyes. Or that weak little smile on his face. It seemed to be a forced smile. As if the man were trying to cover up his true feelings. As if he were trying to hide something.

Hide something. A gun? Maybe he had a hidden gun. Maybe he was trying to get on the airplane to hijack it.

No, that couldn't be. The metal detector would spot a gun and sound a warning. No, he couldn't be a hijacker. He's probably just afraid of flying. A lot of people are.

Still, Linda watched the man closely as he walked up to the metal detector. He *did* look like he was trying to hide something.

The red-haired man took one step forward and suddenly the metal detector started to ring. The man stopped smiling. A guard asked him to go back.

"Put any keys or coins in this pan," the guard said. "They sometimes set off the metal detector. Then walk through again."

Without saying a word, the man put some loose change and a few keys in the pan. He looked just a little worried.

Maybe he *does* have a gun, Linda thought. She watched as the man walked through the metal detector again.

But this time nothing happened.

The man started to smile again. That same strange smile. He picked up his change and his keys and walked off toward the airplane.

I hope he doesn't sit next to me on the plane, Linda thought. He may not be a hijacker, but he is strange. I'd hate to have to ride all the way

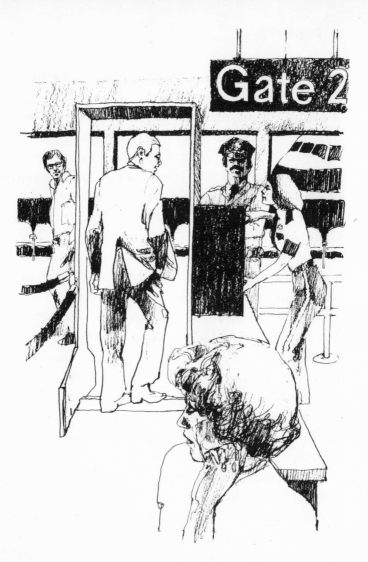

"Fine," said Linda.

The TCA man marked Linda's seat number on her boarding pass and wished her a happy trip.

The waiting room was filled with people. A lot of people would be on TCA Flight 136 to Jamaica. There were only a few empty seats left in the waiting room. Linda spotted one and started over to it, but then she stopped.

The red-haired man was sitting in the seat next to it.

Linda started to look for somewhere else to sit until it was time to go on board the plane.

No, this is silly, she thought. He won't bite me just because I sit next to him. I'll just make it clear that I don't want to talk if he says anything to me.

With that, she sat down next to the red-haired man, pulled a book from her bag, and began reading.

If the man was at all interested in her, he didn't show it. He sat looking straight ahead, that same strange smile on his face.

He was about 25, tall and rather thin. His red hair was cut very short so you could see the skin on the top of his head through it. His blue eyes were bright but cold. Like ice. His arms seemed just a little too long for the light brown coat he was wearing. But his hands were hard and strong.

"Flight 136 is now ready for boarding," the TCA man said. "Those of you holding gold or red boarding passes will board the airplane first. Those of you holding blue boarding passes will board next. Thank you, and no smoking, please."

Linda looked at her boarding pass. It was red. She would be among those getting on the airplane first.

Out of the corner of her eye, she looked at the boarding pass the red-haired man was holding. *Blue.* Good. That means he will be sitting in another part of the plane, in the back. No chance that he will sit next to me.

Off to a good start, Linda thought, as she boarded the plane. Jamaica here I come!

CHAPTER **2**
YOU CAN CALL ME RED

The giant DC-10 was about to take off for the long trip to Jamaica. The jet engines roared and the plane slowly began to roll forward. Now faster and faster. Linda felt herself being pressed into the seat. The nose of the plane began to lift. She felt a bump as the wheels left the ground and the plane headed up into the blue skies.

Below, the airport was growing smaller and smaller. The buildings on the ground looked like toys.

"They don't waste any time taking off," a voice said.

Linda turned to the man sitting in the seat next to her. He was about her age and rather good-looking. "Yes," she said, smiling. "Just like a rocket."

"My name is Al Baker," the young man said.

"I'm Linda Logan."

from Dallas to Jamaica with someone like that for company.

Linda was on her way to Jamaica to visit her married sister Kathy. Kathy, who was a few years older than Linda, lived in Jamaica with her husband David. Kathy and David had moved to Jamaica last year, from Dallas.

David worked for the United Aluminum Company. The head office was in Dallas. But most of the mining was done in Jamaica. When the company needed a new person to head up their mining work, they picked David.

Ever since David and Kathy had moved to Jamaica, Kathy had wanted Linda to visit them. Linda had been saving up for the trip. Her job selling tickets for Trans Continent Airlines didn't pay much. But anyone who worked for TCA got a special price on tickets. That helped a lot. Now Linda was on her way to Jamaica for two weeks' vacation.

After passing through the metal detector, Linda checked in at the airline counter. "I'd like a window seat, if you have one," she told the man at the TCA counter.

"Let's see what we have," he said. "Here's one behind the wing. Seat 26-A. How's that?"

"Going to Jamaica on vacation?" he asked.

"Sort of. My sister and her husband live there. I'm visiting them. How about you?"

"I live there," Al said. "Work on a fishing boat. We take people out deep-sea fishing."

"Sounds like fun."

"It is. But it's like any job—lots of hard work. Some of those fish really put up a fight."

Al told Linda more about his job on the boat. Linda told Al about her job with TCA. It was clear that they enjoyed each other's company. Time passed quickly.

The airplane banked to the right. "Look," said Linda. "The Gulf of Mexico."

Far below, Linda could see the yellow-brown land meet the deep-blue waters of the Gulf of Mexico. The plane was now heading out over the Gulf, leaving the land behind them. They would not see land again until the plane touched down in Jamaica, 1400 miles to the south.

The red-haired man was sitting all the way in the back of the plane. As soon as the plane was over the Gulf, he got up and went over to where a flight attendant was standing. He handed the flight attendant a small piece of paper.

He saw the look of fear and surprise on the flight attendant's face as she read the paper.

The paper said:

> *I have a bomb under my coat, ready to blow us all up.*
>
> *Do just as I tell you. I want to speak to the pilot.*

Opening his coat, the man showed the flight attendant the bomb. He had it tied to his body.

"All I have to do is push this switch. . . ." the man whispered.

"I understand," the flight attendant answered.

"Let's go see the pilot."

They walked to the front of the plane. The flight attendant knocked on the cabin door. "Captain Williams," she said. "Please open the door. I have something very important to tell you."

The door opened and Captain Williams looked out. "Yes, what is it, Miss Holman?"

"This man wants to talk to you," Miss Holman said. "It's important that you see him."

Miss Holman and the red-haired man went into the pilot's cabin. The man opened his coat and showed Captain Williams the bomb. "Don't try anything or I'll blow us all to bits."

"Who are you? What do you want?" the pilot said in an angry voice.

"Who am I? You can call me Red. As for what I want, I want you to do just as I say. My friends and I are taking over your airplane."

"Your friends?" Captain Williams said.

"Yes," said Red, smiling. "Open the cabin door and look."

"Take a look, Miss Holman," the pilot said.

The flight attendant looked out. A man in dark glasses was standing near the door. He looked Miss Holman in the eyes and patted his coat. Then he pointed at a woman sitting a few seats away. She smiled at the flight attendant. A cold, knowing smile.

"The one with the dark glasses is my friend Marco," Red said. "The black-haired woman is my friend Zia. I have two more friends in the center cabin. And all my friends have bombs. . . . Now, Captain, get back in your seat."

Captain Williams sat back down in his seat next to the co-pilot, who had been flying the plane. "I'll take over, Paul," he said to the co-pilot. The Captain turned to Red. "Now what?"

Red sat down in a seat behind the pilot. "Now . . ." he said slowly. "Now I want you to crash this plane into the sea."

"Are you crazy?"

"Not at all. I want you to put the plane into a dive and crash into the sea."

"You must be mad!" the pilot shouted. "I won't do it!"

"Oh yes you will. Because if you don't, my friends and I will blow up the plane."

"What does it matter then how we die?" the pilot said.

"Do as I say and you won't die," Red said.

"What do you mean? I don't understand."

"It's very simple," Red said. "I want you to put the plane into a dive and crash into the sea. At the same time, I want you to radio that you are in trouble and out of control."

"You can't ask me to crash my plane into the sea," Captain Williams said.

"Yes I can," Red said. *"Now do it!"*

CHAPTER **3**

CRASH DIVE

"Must be some bad weather coming up," Al said to Linda. "The Captain has turned on the seat belt sign." When this lighted sign went on, all passengers had to be in their seats and have their seat belts on.

"No sign of any storm," said Linda, looking out the window. "Just lots of blue sky and blue water."

"Maybe he spotted a storm on the radar," said Al, putting on his seat belt.

"Can't be too bumpy," Linda said. "At 39,000 feet, we are above most of the weather. We just . . ."

Before she could finish her sentence, the plane went into a sudden, sharp dive. Someone screamed. Glasses, dishes, books, and other loose things inside the plane went flying.

One of the flight attendants had been making sure everyone was in his seat. She fell to the floor when the plane started to dive. She cried out in pain. She had broken her leg in the fall.

Linda could feel her heart pounding. "What has happened?" she said to Al. "Are we going to crash?"

"I don't know," Al said, just as frightened. "I don't know. Just hold on and hope for the best."

Down, down, down the plane went. The engines of the big DC-10 screamed and pushed the plane toward the sea. In another minute, they would smash into it and be killed.

In the pilot's cabin, Captain Williams held the plane in the dive. *20,000 feet . . . 15,000 feet . . . 12,000 feet . . . 10,000 feet . . .*

The co-pilot was on the radio. "This is TCA Flight 136. We are in trouble. We are out of control. The plane is in a dive. We can't pull out of it. We are heading straight for the sea. . . ."

Down, down. *9,000 feet . . . 8,000 feet . . . 7,000 feet . . . 6,000 feet . . .*

"We don't have much time left!" Captain Williams said to Red. "I've got to pull up or we will crash!"

"Not yet, Captain," said Red, holding one finger on the bomb switch. "Keep diving! Co-pilot, you stay on the radio."

"This is TCA Flight 136. We are out of control over the Gulf. We are out of control and headed for the Gulf. . . ."

5,000 feet . . . 4,000 feet . . . 3,000 feet . . . Captain Williams could see the waves on the sea growing larger as they got closer. *2,000 feet . . . 1,800 feet . . . Too late!*

"Now!" Red shouted. "Pull up, Captain!"

Captain Williams pulled back on the controls as hard as he could. But the plane would not pull up. *1,500 feet . . . 1,200 feet . . .*

"Come on!" the pilot said. "Come on, baby, pull up, pull up." *1,000 feet . . .* The wings on the DC-10 were shaking. He hoped that they would stay on.

"Full power to all engines," Captain Williams said to the co-pilot. "Bring her up! Get her nose up!"

The plane was beginning to pull out of the dive. But would there be enough time? The sea was rushing up to meet them. The plane's engines screamed. The wings shook.

At 500 feet they pulled out of the dive.

"Radio that we are all right, Paul," Captain Williams said to the co-pilot.

"No," said Red. "You're not going to radio anything to anyone. Remember, I still have this bomb."

Red pulled a map from his coat and handed it to the Captain. "Keep the plane at 500 feet and follow the course on this map."

Captain Williams looked at the map and then at Red. "Belize?" he said. "This is a map of Belize. What do you want me to do with it?"

"Use it to fly there with," Red answered. "Because that's where we are going. To Belize, Central America. Change course right now."

"Not until you tell me what's going on," Captain Williams said. "I have the lives of my passengers to think about."

"First change course for Belize. Then I'll tell you everything you need to know." Red's finger was back on the bomb switch again.

Captain Williams studied the map Red had given him. To reach Belize, he would have to fly straight south across the Gulf of Mexico. Past the Yucatan Peninsula. Then turn a bit to the west. But where would he land? Belize was a land of thick jungle. You can't land a DC-10 in the jungle. What were the hijackers planning to do when the plane reached Belize?

"All right," said Captain Williams. "We are now on course for Belize."

"Good," said Red. "Just keep doing what I say and no one will get hurt."

"Get *hurt!*" said Miss Holman, the flight attendant. "We almost got *killed* because of that dive you forced us to make."

"The dive was necessary," Red answered. "A part of our plan. We had to make it look like the plane really was crashing. And that's just how it looked on the radar that was tracking this plane. A sudden dive from 39,000 feet. A radio call saying the plane is out of control. They follow you on radar until you are too low to be picked up. Everyone thinks the plane has smashed into the sea. They try to reach you by radio—like they are trying to do now. But no answer."

"But we didn't crash," said Miss Holman.

"Of course not," Red answered. "But it looks like you did. That's the important thing. They check the radar. But we are flying too low now to be picked up by radar. What happened? The plane must have crashed. They are probably already sending out planes and ships to look for anyone who might have lived through the crash. They will be looking for us around the spot the plane went off the radar. But we won't be there. We will be on our way to the jungles of Belize."

Back in the passengers cabin, Marco and the other hijackers had taken over. "Just stay in your seats and nothing will happen to you," Marco said. "My friends and I would hate to have to blow up this airplane."

"What do you want with us?" one of the passengers said. "Why did you hijack the plane?"

"You'll find out soon enough," Marco said. "Just sit back and enjoy the ride. And remember that each of us has a bomb. So don't try anything."

Al turned to Linda. "How do you suppose they got on board carrying bombs?" he whispered. "Every passenger had to go through a metal detector."

"Metal detectors are only good for spotting metal—things like guns," Linda whispered back. "Their bombs must not have any metal in them."

Miss Holman was helping the flight attendant who had broken her leg. Other flight attendants were trying to keep the passengers from becoming too frightened. But there were only four flight attendants. And there were almost 200 passengers.

Miss Holman was putting a thin board on the flight attendant's broken leg to keep it stiff. Linda was sitting only a few seats away. "Is there anything I can do to help?" she asked the flight attendant.

The flight attendant looked up. "Oh, thanks, but I don't think so. Against company rules," she answered.

"But it wouldn't be against the rules," Linda said. "I work for TCA."

"Well, we *could* use some help. We were short-handed to begin with. And now that Jackie has broken her leg. . . ."

Linda was just getting out of her seat when Marco spotted her. "You there! Get back in your seat!" he shouted. He went for her and was about to hit her in the face. Miss Holman stepped between them. "Stop!" she said. "Keep your hands off her. She works for TCA. She is going to help us with the passengers."

"Says who?" Marco said. "I told you that no one was to leave their seats!"

Zia, the woman hijacker, came up to Marco. "Cut it out, Marco," she said. "Remember, the Boss said not to hurt anyone if you didn't have to. The flight attendants do need help. Let the girl help them."

"Well, OK," Marco said. "But I'm going to keep my eye on her. You better, too."

The two hijackers went back to where they were standing before.

"Thanks," Linda said to the flight attendant. "He's a mean one. Now, what can I do to help?"

"Help me get Jackie to the back of the plane, if you would. By the way, my name is Pat Holman. What's yours?"

"Linda. Linda Logan."

The plane was still flying only 500 feet above the water. Captain Williams wanted to bring it up, but Red wouldn't let him.

"We stay at 500 feet," Red said. "Below any radar that could pick us up."

"But 500 feet is too low to be safe," the pilot said.

Red laughed. "Safe enough if you are a good enough pilot. Hold it at 500 feet."

Paul Zenner, the co-pilot, tapped Captain Williams on the arm. "Look," he said. "Land coming up. We must be nearing Belize."

There was no sign of any town. All they could see was thick green jungle.

"It doesn't look like anyone lives there," the co-pilot said.

"Not many people do," said Red. "That's one reason we are coming here."

"And where do you think I'm going to land the plane?" said Captain Williams. "I can't land this thing in the middle of the jungle. A DC-10 isn't a helicopter, you know."

"Just keep to the course on the map. You may be surprised," Red answered.

The big plane was over the land now, flying close to the tops of the trees. There was still no sign of any town—or any airport.

"Over there!" the co-pilot said, pointing to the right. "Looks like smoke coming up from the jungle.

"Head for it," Red ordered. "My friends on the ground must have heard our engines. They are making smoke to show us the way."

"Friends?" Captain Williams asked. "You mean there are more of you?"

"Oh yes," Red told him. "We even have our own airport. An old army landing field built during World War II. No one has used it since the war ended. The jungle grew over most of it and people just forgot it was there. We cut away the jungle and cleared the field so you could land there."

"I can't land a DC-10 on a World War II landing field," Captain Williams said. "There isn't enough room."

"It will be a little tight," Red answered. "But there is enough room. Just enough. We have this whole thing planned. We know what we are doing."

Captain Williams could see the old landing field now. The field had been cleared of jungle. But it was very short for a plane the size of a DC-10. He wondered if he could make it without crashing.

On one side of the field were some old army buildings. Three men were standing by a burning oil drum in front of the buildings. Black smoke from the burning oil streamed up into the blue afternoon sky. The three men watched as the big plane made a circle over the field. The pilot was getting ready to land.

Captain Williams turned on the seat belt sign and told the passengers they were about to land. "This will be a tight landing," he said. "Put your heads down and bend forward. Fold your arms in front of you."

Linda came back to her seat for the landing. "How is it going?" Al asked her.

"I'll let you know when we land," she answered. "After we find out who these hijackers are and what they want."

Captain Williams made one more pass over the field. Now he was ready to land. He cut back on the engines and checked all his controls.

"Wheels?" he said to the co-pilot.

"Locked in place."

"Flaps?"

"All flaps full."

"Air speed?"

"165."

"Then here we go," the pilot said. "It's got to be right the first time."

The wheels of the plane touched down on the far end of the field. Would there be enough room to stop in time? Captain Williams hit the brakes as hard as he could. He also reversed his engines to slow the plane.

The brakes soon began to smoke. Would they last long enough to stop the plane? Captain Williams could see a wall of jungle at the end of the field. If they couldn't stop in time, they would smash into the jungle and be killed.

CHAPTER 4
THE RIVER

The brakes on the wheels of the DC-10 screamed and smoked. They were almost gone. But they held long enough to bring the plane to a stop. It had been close. The jungle at the end of the landing field was less than 100 feet from the nose of the stopped plane.

As soon as the plane stopped, the men who had been standing by the old army buildings came running over. Each one carried a machine gun. Zia opened the door of the plane and put out the steps. One of the armed men came running up. The man opened a bag he had with him and took out some more machine guns. Zia gave one to each of the hijackers on the plane.

Al watched as Zia came over to give Marco a gun. "First bombs. Now machine guns," he whispered to Linda. "We are done for if someone doesn't do something fast."

"Like what?" Linda said.

"Like this!" Al shouted, jumping up and grabbing Marco by the neck. But Marco was as strong as a bear, and just as mean. He broke free from Al's hold and smashed the machine gun into Al's body as hard as he could. Al fell to the floor and lay still.

"I should fill you full of holes!" Marco said. He pointed the machine gun at Al's head. "You got it coming!"

"Don't shoot him!" Linda cried. "Leave him alone!"

"*You* again!" Marco shouted, pointing the machine gun at Linda. "I'll be happy to kill you, too."

"Stop it!" It was Red. He walked over to Marco and pushed the gun down. "Get hold of yourself. No gun play unless you have to. Go keep an eye on the pilot. I'll take care of this."

Red helped Al back into his seat. Al opened his eyes but was still having trouble seeing straight. He checked to see if anything was broken.

Red said, "That was not a very smart thing to do. Marco is a very dangerous man. He likes to hurt people. Remember that. If you try anything funny again, I may let him shoot you. Or I may shoot you myself. Got it?"

Red turned and walked back to the pilot's cabin. Captain Williams was waiting for him. "I want to know what is going on," the pilot said. "Why did you hijack us?"

Red smiled. "Very simple," he said. "We hijacked you for money. We want ten million dollars for your safe return."

"You'll never get away with it," Captain Williams said.

"Oh, I think we will," the hijacker said. "Remember that no one knows where you and your airplane are. Everyone thought you crashed into the ocean. No one will think of looking for you in the jungles of Belize."

"And now you are going to radio TCA that you are holding us?" Captain Williams asked.

"Yes," said Red. "But not on the plane's radio. Too easy to trace the call and find out where you are. We have our own low-power radio that can't be traced. We also have a fishing boat out in the Gulf of Mexico. We will radio the fishing boat. The boat will relay the call with their own radio. That way no one can trace us."

"But they can still trace the fishing boat," Captain Williams said.

"I don't think so," Red said. "There are hundreds of fishing boats in the Gulf. How will anyone know which boat is ours? And to make sure the calls are not traced, the boat will keep moving. It will never radio a call from the same spot twice."

"And what if TCA won't pay you the ten million dollars? Have you thought of that?" Captain Williams said.

"We mean business. If we don't get the money in 48 hours, we will blow up the plane and kill everyone. If we do get the money, we will let you go. We will tell TCA to put the money in a can and drop it at a certain spot in the Gulf. Our boat will pick it up. As soon as we get a radio call from the boat saying that they have the money, we will let you go."

While Red and Captain Williams were talking, the co-pilot was slowly moving his hand up to the radio switch. If he could turn on the radio, he might be able to call for help. Slowly, his hand moved toward the radio. Another inch and he could turn it on.

Marco's machine gun went off with a flash and a roar. The co-pilot cried out and fell over, blood streaming from his arm. The radio was smashed.

"I told you not to try anything," Marco shouted, training his gun on the pilot. "Your co-pilot should have known better."

"Paul!" Captain Williams shouted, rushing over to the co-pilot.

"My arm," the co-pilot said. "Help me get . . ."

"Don't try to talk," Captain Williams said. "I'll help you. You'll be OK if I can stop the blood."

Red grabbed Marco and pushed him against the cabin wall. "I told you no gun play!" he shouted at the man. "You really do like to hurt people, don't you! Get off this plane before you kill someone! Get off and go help the others with the radio!"

Marco said nothing. He just looked at Red through his dark glasses. If he was afraid of Red, he didn't show it. But he did as he was told.

Red called for Zia. "Tell one of the flight attendants to come up here with some clean cloth. A man has been hurt."

Then the hijacker turned to the pilot. "You had better tell the passengers what is happening. Tell them everything. About the ten million dollars. And about your co-pilot. I want them to know that we mean business. We will kill you if we have to."

When the pilot had finished talking to the passengers, Linda turned to Al. "Do you think they really will let us go if they get the money?"

"No telling," Al answered. "Once they get the money, they won't need us. But we are in the middle of the jungle. We could be here a long time before help reaches us. In this jungle heat, things could get pretty bad. The co-pilot needs a doctor, too."

Just then, Pat Holman walked up. "Linda," she said. "Could you help us again? The passengers are very frightened. We are going to serve them some food. That may make them feel a little better."

Pat and Linda went to the back of the plane. "Where is the food cooked?" Linda asked, looking around.

"Below," Pat answered. "Come on, I'll show you." She pressed a button and a small door opened.

"What's this?" Linda asked.

"An elevator," the flight attendant answered. "It goes to the kitchen, below. We cook the food there. Then we bring it up to serve. Get on. There is only room for one at a time on the elevator. I'll follow you."

Linda took the elevator to the kitchen below. It was a small but complete kitchen. There was a sink in one corner. There were three stoves along one wall. Dishes of food were stored along the other wall. Next to the food, there was a little round window with a red handle below it. Looking out, Linda could see the hijackers walking around under the plane.

Pat stepped out of the elevator. "Like our kitchen?" she asked.

Linda pointed to the window and the handle. "Is this a door to the outside?" she asked.

"Not really," Pat said. "Just an opening we use to put food on the plane at the airport."

"But someone could get out this way!" Linda said in a whisper. "Someone could get out and go for help."

"It would be too dangerous," Pat said. "There are hijackers outside watching the plane. Come on, let's get these dinners ready."

When they came up on the elevator, Zia was waiting. "What were you two talking about?" Zia said. "Not planning anything, I hope."

"Just fixing the food," Pat said.

"Well, cut out the talk," Zia said.

Pat and Linda served the dinners and went back to the kitchen for more.

"Pat," Linda whispered. "We have to try to escape. Someone has to go for help. We can get out through this door."

"I can't go," Pat said. "I have to stay here and look after the passengers. In this heat, they are going to need all the help I can give them."

"Well, then I'll go," Linda said.

"You'll be killed if you try it," Pat said. "What good would that do any of us? No, I can't let you."

Zia called down. "I said to cut out the talk. Get up here, both of you!"

"We're bringing the food up now," Pat called back. "Just a minute."

She turned to Linda. "Forget about trying to escape. It's too dangerous. Come on, now, before Zia decides to come down here herself. With her machine gun."

After the food was served, Linda went back to her seat. By now it was night. But the heat inside the plane was as bad as ever. People tried to rest or sleep. But sleep did not come easy.

Linda sat in her seat, waiting. She could hear the hijackers outside the plane talking. They were standing around their radio, waiting for a call from the fishing boat. After an hour or so, some of them went off to bed, taking the radio inside one of the old buildings. Linda looked out the window. She could not see anyone. Maybe they had all gone to bed.

She got up from her seat and walked to the back of the plane. One of the hijackers was standing there. He was a big ugly man with a red face. Linda did not know his name.

"What do you want back here?" the man said. "Get back to your seat."

"I'm helping the flight attendants," Linda said.

"I know," the red-faced man said. "But dinner is over."

"One of the passengers has a baby. The baby needs some milk," Linda lied. "I'm going down to the kitchen to get it for her."

"I said dinner is over. The baby will have to wait until morning. Get back to your seat."

Linda was thinking of what to try next. Just then a baby started crying. What a bit of luck, Linda thought.

She turned and started back to her seat. "All right," she told the hijacker. "If you want to hear that baby crying all night for its milk. . . ."

The hijacker grabbed her by the arm. "Wait a minute. OK, you can get the milk. Just shut that kid up."

Linda pushed the button for the elevator and went down to the kitchen. She looked out the little window. No one around. Behind the old army buldings she could see a river. If she could get across the river, she might be able to find help.

She turned the handle under the window. The small door opened. Linda looked out. It was about 15 feet to the ground. A long drop. But there was no other way. She let herself down by her hands and then dropped to the ground.

Linda hit the ground and rolled. The fall knocked the wind out of her, but she was not hurt. Nothing broken. She looked around. There were lights in one building, but she could see no one.

Slowly she got up and made her way toward the river. To get there she had to go right past the army buildings. She tried to make as little noise as possible. She could feel her heart pounding.

Suddenly there was a voice from inside the building. "Who's out there?" the voice said. "Who is it?"

The voice belonged to Marco.

Linda stopped where she was. It was very dark. Maybe he wouldn't see her. The door of the building opened and Marco stepped out holding his machine gun. "Who's there?" he shouted. He brought his gun up and got ready to fire.

Linda knew she had to act. She jumped forward and started running for the river as fast as she could.

Marco spotted her and fired. The bullets kicked up dirt behind her, but missed.

"So it's you again!" Marco shouted. "I don't know how you got out of the plane. But you are going to be sorry you did!" He fired again. This time the shots were closer. Linda could hear them going by her head.

She did not stop when she reached the river. She hit the water with a splash and began swimming for the other side. Marco fired again. The bullets splashed up water all around her.

"Get ready to die!" Marco screamed.

Linda went under and kept swimming. For a minute Marco couldn't spot her. He fired again, but he wasn't sure where she was.

Linda came up, still swimming hard. She was almost to the other side of the river. Another few feet and she would be there.

But Marco had spotted her again. "Say goodbye to the world!" he screamed. He had Linda in the sights of his machine gun. This time he wouldn't miss. Marco's face was filled with hate. He fired.

But nothing happened. Marco's gun had jammed. Linda pulled herself out of the water and ran into the black jungle.

Marco wasn't going to let the girl escape. He dived into the water holding the jammed machine gun over his head. "I'll fix this on the other side," he said. "And then I'm coming after you. Do you think you can run faster than me? Do you think you can escape from Marco?"

He laughed in a mad way. "Marco is coming after you!" he shouted. "You are going to die!"

CHAPTER **5**

IN THE JUNGLE

Linda could not see where she was going. But it was not important. She had only one thought: to get away from Marco. She pushed her way through the thick jungle, running as fast as she could. Her clothes were torn. There were cuts on her hands and face from the sharp jungle plants. But she knew she had to keep moving. She could hear Marco fighting his way through the jungle behind her. And he was getting closer.

Linda was very tired. And she felt sick from the jungle heat. But unless she could run even faster she knew Marco would soon catch up. She rushed on, pushing the jungle plants out of her way. But suddenly she tripped and fell.

She was about to get up and start running again. Then she stopped. *Get hold of yourself,* she thought. *Stop and think.* She was shaking all over.

Linda could hear Marco crashing about in the jungle. *He can't see any better than you can,* she told herself. *He's following you by sound.*

Linda was right. Now Marco stopped and listened. Linda lay still. Suddenly there was a sharp crash of machine gun fire. Linda hit the dirt but didn't move. *He's just trying to frighten me into running again,* she thought. *He's too far away to hit me with that gun. And he doesn't know for sure where I am.*

Linda slowly got back up and began moving again. This time very quietly. After ten minutes she stopped to rest. She heard the sound of Marco's gun again. But this time the sound was not as close. She was getting away.

She kept going for another hour. At last she felt she was safe. By now Linda was too tired to take another step. She lay down at the foot of a giant jungle tree and was soon sleeping.

The strange cry of a jungle bird woke Linda early the next morning. She looked around. Tall jungle trees on all sides. Only a little of the light from the sun could get through. Everything was deep green.

She decided to circle back toward the river. The night before, she had seen a boat tied up near the army buildings. A boat must mean that the river goes somewhere. To a town or a farm. Or maybe the ocean. But somewhere.

Linda planned to walk back to the river, but stay away from the landing field. She would follow the river until she found someone to help. Then she could tell the police or the army about the hijackers.

She had taken only a few steps when she heard something. She stopped and hid behind a tree. She heard the noise again. Closer.

Linda took a quick look from around the tree.

Marco!

He was only a few hundred feet away. He had been following her tracks all night. Linda knew she had to act fast. She slipped away from the trees and moved deeper into the jungle. She was trying not to make any noise. But she stepped on a stick and Marco heard her.

There was only one thing to do now: run. Linda set off through the jungle as fast as she could. But Marco was right behind her. She was running as hard as she could. But Marco was catching up.

All at once Linda found herself in an open clearing. She looked around. No place to hide. She had to get across the clearing and back into the trees.

But before she could make it, Marco had caught up. He shouted at her to stop. Linda turned and saw him standing on one side of the clearing. His machine gun was pointed right at her. This time he couldn't miss.

Linda tried to reason with him. "Don't shoot," she cried. "You win. I'm sorry I tried to escape. I'll go back with you. You don't have to shoot me."

"You're right," said Marco. "I don't have to shoot you. But I'm going to. You have caused me too much trouble. I might as well shoot you now as when we catch the tuna."

Marco was about to fire. Suddenly there was a loud bang from across the clearing. Marco screamed and fell over.

Linda turned and saw a man holding a smoking gun. He stepped forward into the clearing, keeping the gun on Marco. But Marco was no danger now.

The man walked over to Marco and looked at him.

"Is he dead?" Linda asked.

The man turned. "No," he answered. "But he's hurt bad."

"He was going to kill me," Linda said.

"I know. I saw the whole thing. There was nothing else I could do. I had to shoot him to save you. Here, take his machine gun. We will bring him to my camp. We may be able to save his life yet."

Linda watched as the man picked Marco up. "Follow me," he said to Linda.

Linda was still too surprised and frightened to say much. They walked for a while before Linda asked the man who he was.

"I was just about to ask you the same thing," the man answered. "I'm Dan Evans. I'm head of Mayan Studies at Hamilton College. I'm down here looking for Mayan ruins."

"Mayan ruins?" Linda asked. "Then why the gun?"

"Oh, that," Dan Evans answered. "There is big money selling things from Mayan ruins. It's against the law of course. But bandits don't care. They wait until we find something interesting. Then they move in. They kill anyone who gets in their way. No police to worry about in the jungle. That's why I carry this gun. Because of bandits."

"Have you had much trouble with bandits?" Linda asked. Hijackers *and* bandits, she thought. That would be too much.

"Not this trip. The bandits don't know we are here yet. There are just three of us in the party. If we find any good ruins, we will come back later with more people to dig them up. Now, tell me who you are. And tell me why this man was trying to kill you."

Linda told him the whole story, about the hijacking, about her escape from the plane, and about Marco. "We have to do something," she said. "We have to tell the police or the army. If we don't, the hijackers may kill all the passengers."

By this time, they were nearing Dan Evans' camp. Two other men were standing there. "What's happening, Dan?" said one of the men, running over to him.

"Trouble," Dan answered.

"Bandits?"

"Worse than that," Dan said. "Give me a hand and I'll tell you all about it."

They carried Marco inside a tent. There was blood all over his chest. His eyes were closed and he could not speak. Dan looked him over.

"He's weak," Dan said. "I don't know if he is going to make it."

"Let me look at him," the other man said. "I once studied to be a doctor. I may be able to help him."

"OK, Charley, see what you can do," Dan said.

Charley opened Marco's shirt. "Bad," he said. "Pretty bad. Get me some hot water."

The third man looked into the tent. "I'll get the water," he said.

"Thanks, Chip," Charley said.

They worked on Marco for an hour. He had lost a lot of blood. But he didn't seem to be getting any worse. "With luck, he will live," Charley said at last. "I've done about all I can do for him."

While they were taking care of Marco, Linda washed up and rested. Her heart was still pounding and she felt like she wanted to throw up.

Later, Dan came over. "Feeling better?" he asked.

"A little," Linda answered. "I'm still shaking. Thanks for saving my life."

"You had a very close call."

"What are we going to do about those hijackers?" Linda asked.

"We have a radio," Dan said. "I called the army while you were resting. They are on their way."

"Great," Linda said. "When will they get here?"

"Not until late this afternoon. They have to come all the way from Belize City, almost 50 miles from here."

"That's not so far. They could use helicopters."

"We talked about that," Dan answered. "But there is no place to land. The jungle is too thick. And the hijackers would hear the helicopters coming. If they thought they were trapped, they might blow up the plane. So the army is coming by boat. There is a river near our camp. They will come by boat up this river."

"Is that the same river that goes past the landing field?" Linda asked.

"No, that is a small stream that leads to the ocean. This is another river. It goes to Belize City."

Chip came up. He was carrying a radio on his back. "Are you ready, Dan?" he asked.

"Just about," Dan answered. "I want to make sure that Linda is all right before we go."

"What are you going to do?" Linda asked.

"Chip and I are going to the landing field," Dan said. "We are going to try to find out what the hijackers are up to. Maybe we can pick up their radio calls to the fishing boat. If we can, we will listen in. We will try to find out what they plan to do."

"I'm coming with you," Linda said, forgetting her fear.

"No," said Dan. "It's too dangerous. You stay here and help Charley. We will be back later."

"It's no more dangerous for me than for you," Linda said. "I'm coming with you. Don't forget, those hijackers hijacked *me,* not you. I want to make sure they don't get away."

"She has a point, Dan," said Chip.

"Well, then, let's get started," Dan said, picking up his pack and gun.

CHAPTER **6**

A SIGNAL FROM SEA ROVER

"Try again," Red told Zia. Red and another hijacker stood by the radio as Zia tried again to reach the fishing boat. They were using a low-power radio so their signals couldn't be traced. But because of the low power, their signals were weak.

Zia sat by the radio key and tapped out a message in Morse Code. F-L-Y-I-N-G F-I-S-H T-O S-E-A R-O-V-E-R . . . C-O-M-E I-N . . .

The hijackers had moved the radio outside for a better signal. But they were still having trouble reaching the fishing boat, *Sea Rover*.

"Keep trying," Red said. The hijackers had been trying to reach the *Sea Rover* since morning. They had not heard from the fishing boat since last night.

"Maybe something has happened to them," said the man standing next to Red. He wiped his ugly red face on his shirt. He was the hijacker who had let Linda into the kitchen for milk.

"Nothing has happened to them, Oscar," Red said. "Our signal is a little weak, that's all."

But Oscar was worried. "I don't know," he said. "What if the Coast Guard found out about the *Sea Rover?* Maybe the Coast Guard got the boat."

"Enough of that," Red said in an angry voice. "Everything is all right."

"All right, is it?" Oscar said, wiping his face again. "Is the escape of the girl all right? And what about Marco? What has happened to Marco?"

"There is nothing to worry about," Red went on. "Marco will be back as soon as he has finished his business. He likes to take his time when he does something like this. Don't worry about the girl getting away. And don't worry about Marco."

"I still don't like it," Oscar said.

"Try the radio again, Zia," Red said.

Zia tapped out the same message.

F-L-Y-I-N-G   F-I-S-H   T-O   S-E-A
R-O-V-E-R . . . C-O-M-E   I-N . . .

This time there was an answer. A weak signal.
S-E-A   R-O-V-E-R   T-O   F-L-Y-I-N-G
F-I-S-H . . . W-E   R-E-A-D   Y-O-U . . .
A-L-L   O-K?

Zia tapped back. A-L-L   O-K   H-E-R-E
. . . H-O-W   I-S   T-H-E   F-I-S-H-I-N-G?

The *Sea Rover* radioed back. W-E   H-A-V-E
P-U-T   O-U-T   T-H-E   B-A-I-T . . . N-O
B-I-T-E-S   Y-E-T . . . W-I-L-L   L-E-T
Y-O-U   K-N-O-W   I-F   W-E   C-A-T-C-H
W-H-A-T   W-E   A-R-E   L-O-O-K-I-N-G
F-O-R . . .

Zia looked up at Red. "How shall I answer?"
she asked.

Red said, "Tell them that we are looking for
one kind of fish only. Tell them to radio us as
soon as they catch that kind of fish."

Zia tapped out the message.

In the jungle across from the landing field,
Dan, Chip, and Linda were listening on their
own radio.

"It's a good thing for us they had trouble
reaching the fishing boat," Chip said. "That
gave me enough time to find their signal on our
radio."

"Do you think the Coast Guard is also picking them up?" Linda asked.

"Maybe," Chip answered. "But even if they are, they wouldn't know it's the hijackers. It would just sound like two fishing boats talking about fishing. *Sea Rover* and *Flying Fish.*"

"*Flying Fish,*" said Dan. "Some fishing boat —a DC-10!"

The DC-10 sat at the far end of the landing field. The door was open. A hijacker with a machine gun was standing by it. Other hijackers were on the ground and under the wings. They were putting something on the bottom of the plane.

"What are they doing?" Linda asked. Now the hijackers were running a long wire from the plane to the army buildings.

"Oh no!" said Dan. "It looks like they are getting ready to blow up the plane. Those things they are putting on are bombs!"

"We have to do something!" Linda said.

"The army will be here soon. Charley will show them the way," Dan said.

"But remember what you said," Linda whispered. "You said the hijackers might blow up the plane if they thought they were trapped.

You were right. If the army moves in, they are sure to blow up the plane."

No one said anything for a minute. They watched the hijackers moving around on the landing field. They could see Red, Zia, and Oscar by the radio waiting for a message from the *Sea Rover.*

Suddenly there was a noise behind them in the jungle. Dan grabbed his gun. "Keep down," he said to Chip and Linda. "I'm going to see what that noise was." He moved off into the jungle toward the noise.

Linda listened but could hear nothing. Just the cries of a jungle bird. Five minutes passed.

Linda looked around for some sign of Dan. But there was nothing to be seen. Nothing but the green jungle plants.

Suddenly the leaves parted. There was the face of a man holding a machine gun. Linda's heart jumped.

There was another man behind him. It was Dan.

"It's OK," Dan whispered. "This is Captain Olmedo of the army. Sorry I took so long. I was helping Captain Olmedo get his men in place."

"I didn't want them to get too close yet," Captain Olmedo explained. "Mr. Evans told me about the bombs on the plane. I don't want the hijackers to know the army is here. Not until we have a plan on how to free the passengers."

"Maybe we could trick them into leaving the plane," Linda said. "If we could get them away from it for just a few minutes, the army could rush them."

"No," said Captain Olmedo. "They would set off the bombs before we even got close."

Chip was thinking. "Maybe we could trick them another way."

"Such as?" Captain Olmedo asked.

"If I turn the power on our radio way down, the signal becomes very weak," Chip explained. "It would sound like it's coming from a long way off. We could send a message saying we were the *Sea Rover*. We could tell them we had picked up the money. Then we could tell them to make their get-away."

"But they would know it wasn't the *Sea Rover*," Captain Olmedo said. "They would know because your voice is different."

"No, they wouldn't," Chip said. "They are sending in Morse Code. Just dots and dashes. No voices."

"It might work," Dan said. "But there is one thing we don't know. And without that, the plan won't work. You remember that the hijackers radioed that they were looking for just one kind of fish. That one kind of fish is their code-word. It is the code-word for the ten million dollars they want. And only the hijackers know that code-word. It could be any kind of fish. . . ."

"Right," said Chip. "And if we used the wrong code-word, they would know the message didn't really come from the *Sea Rover*."

"I think I know what the code-word is," Linda said.

"What? How?" said Dan.

"Just before Marco was going to shoot me, he said something," Linda answered. "Something strange. But I was too frightened then to think about it."

"What did he say?" Dan asked.

"Marco said, 'I might as well shoot you now as when we catch the tuna.' *Catch the tuna*. Tuna must be the code-word for the money."

"I think you're right," Dan said. "Let's try it."

"I'll get the rest of my men in place," Captain Olmedo said. "I want most of them by the stream. If your plan works, the hijackers will probably use that boat of theirs to get away."

When everything was ready, Chip switched the radio to 'Send.' He turned the power way down so his signal was very weak. Then he sent the message. S–E–A R–O–V–E–R T–O F–L–Y–I–N–G F–I–S–H . . . W–E H–A–V–E

C-A-U-G-H-T T-H-E T-U-N-A...Y-O-U
C-A-N C-O-M-E H-O-M-E ...

Linda could see the hijackers talking and laughing. They believed the radio message. She could hear Red calling to the hijackers on the plane. He was telling them to get ready to leave.

"We got the message we were waiting for," Red called. "The *Sea Rover* has caught the tuna! Come on. Let's go!"

Red waited till all the hijackers were in the boat. Zia asked about Marco. Red said they couldn't wait. They had to leave him behind. Then he went over to the radio and shot it to pieces with his machine gun. He didn't want the pilot to call for help until the hijackers were far away.

Zia started the engine of the boat and Red jumped in.

Captain Olmedo waited for just the right time. Then he jumped up and shouted, "This is the army! Throw down your guns! We are all around you!"

The hijackers began firing. Captain Olmedo told his men to return the fire. It was all over in a few minutes. After a few of the hijackers were hit, the others started giving up. They threw down their guns and put up their hands.

But not Red. He jumped from the boat and ran for the wire to the bombs. He was going to blow up the plane!

"Stop or I'll shoot!" Captain Olmedo cried. "Stop!"

But Red kept on. He had only a few more feet to go when Captain Olmedo fired. Red fell to the ground, both legs smashed by machine gun fire.

Then all was quiet. Two army men came over and carried Red away. Others were rounding up the rest of the hijackers.

Dan turned to Captain Olmedo. "What about the *Sea Rover?* Won't it get away?"

"The Coast Guard is looking for the boat now," Captain Olmedo said. "The *Sea Rover* won't get far. As soon as the men on board try to radio their friends here, we will trace their signal. We will take them by surprise, too. Let's go over to the plane and see how the pilot and passengers are doing."

The pilot, Captain Williams, came out to talk to them. Dan told him the whole story of how they had been saved. "And we couldn't have done it without Linda," Dan said, smiling. "She is a very brave person."

"You should get a big reward for this," Captain Williams said. "I'm sure that TCA will think so, too."

"Well, I wouldn't mind some of the tuna the hijackers were talking about," Linda said.

"Tuna? You mean the ten million dollars?!" said Dan, very surprised.

"No," Linda laughed. *"Tuna.* Real tuna. I haven't had anything to eat since yesterday. All of a sudden I'm very hungry."

They all laughed. "Let's take care of that right now," said Captain Williams. "A first-class TCA meal served by the pilot himself."